the FREEDOM
of Being YOURSELF

Getting Your

Identity from

Your Creator

RAY GILDER

Introduction

The concepts in this little book have been burning my heart for several years. I had begun working on this book when I was encouraged by a close friend to produce a book on bivocational ministry first. I set aside this project and started working on *Uniquely Bivocational* which was published in 2013. My role as Bivocational/Small Church Ministries Director for the Tennessee Baptist Convention (April 1995-April 2015) and as National Coordinator for the Bivocational and Small Church Leadership Network (2006-Present) gave me abundant resources and experiences to put together a book with practical helps for a bivocational pastor. That book has literally gone all over the United States. I have been greatly rewarded by the many positive comments sent to me from bivo pastors across the country.

At the completion of the previous book, I returned to working on the subject that has so much meaning to me as an individual. Much of what you will find in the following pages is either autobiographical or the result of experiences I have had. *The Freedom of Being Yourself* contains simple principles of living your life as God designed you to be. I have witnessed hundreds, if not thousands, of individuals who have such a negative attitude toward themselves and the life they lead that they have a difficult time believing God is interested in them or has a plan for their life.

Satan has been quite successful in causing many people to believe that they are insignificant in the Divine design of this universe. When God made this world, He did not have any spare parts left when He finished. You were in His plan from before creation. Imagine what a wonderful world we would have if everyone was tuned in to their Maker and functioning as He designed!

It is my prayer that as you read these pages you will discover the freedom which comes when you are just yourself to the glory of God. We are told that every star in the universe is unique. We would have a much brighter world if every child of God realized that he is a light to his corner of the world. By the time you finish reading this book, I trust you will have discovered the freedom of being yourself.

– Dedication –

This book is dedicated to all those children of God who struggle with feelings of insignificance, inferiority or incompetence and who fail to realize that they are the apple of God's eye. Just like in the story of Cinderella, God's glass slipper fits your foot!

the FREEDOM of Being YOURSELF

By Ray Gilder - ©2016 Ray Gilder. All rights reserved.

Book cover and inside design: Royce DeGrie, degriephoto.com
Cover Photo: tunart (iStockphoto)
Printed by Pollock Printing, Nashville, Tennessee

ISBN 978-1-944788-04-9 Paperback

Table of Contents

WHO ARE YOU?

Chapter I
Do You Know Who You Are?

Do you know who you are? This is not a discussion about your name, genealogy, age, address or occupation. Who are you deep down inside? If you do not know who you are, it is doubtful that anyone else does.

Previous hurts and disappointments have caused most of us to withdraw into a shell like a turtle. In our attempts to protect ourselves from being hurt or disappointed again, we forfeit the potential of living life to its fullest. One of the most freeing experiences a person can have is to decide to be who you are, to the best of your ability, to the glory of God.

Who you are is not determined by what others think or say you are. We are so quick to judge other people and jump to conclusions before we know all the facts. Everything we experience is channeled through our personal filter system which has a built-in bias toward previous conclusions. It would be extremely beneficial if everyone practiced better listening and communication skills and delayed judgment until all the facts are known.

It is amazing how stories change while being passed from one person to the next. We used to play a game at our youth fellowships called "Gossip." We would sit in a circle and someone would begin by whispering a statement containing several details in the ear of the person next to him. It would then be repeated around the circle. The last person to hear, would stand and tell what he had heard. It was always funny to discover how twisted the statement became as it moved throughout the group. This is a humorous way of helping us realize that things can become very distorted when passed from one person to the next.

Even our families do not know us fully. A frequent hurt among family members is the feeling of not being understood. The Apostle Peter tells men to dwell with their wives according to knowledge (I Peter 3:7). This means that men need to become lifelong students of their wives. If that is true in a marriage where couples spend almost every day together, how much more do we need to try to understand others with whom we relate?

Therefore, you can never base your identity on what others think or say about you. This has more to do with your reputation which you can influence but never fully control. You do not need to be asking others who you are; they need to be asking you that question.

In trying to identify who you are, you must choose to be honest with yourself. The Bible warns us about deceiving ourselves (I Corinthians 3:18, Galatians 6:3, James 1:22, I John 1:8). It is easy for us to think that we are someone or something that we are not. For many people, life is more like a charade than it is a real live performance. Sometimes we try to be who we want to be rather than who we really are.

While all of us can be inspired by the life of someone else, we make a serious mistake when we try to become that person. As children we spent a lot of time dressing up and acting like Spiderman, Superman or Tarzan. Many of us carry that over into adulthood as we choose other heroes to imitate.

The real you is the person God made you to be and that He knows you are. A key concept in knowing who you are is the realization that you are one-of-a-kind. There is no one exactly like you. God is the Master Designer and He made only one of you. Everything in your past, genealogy, culture, experiences and relationships have come together to make you the unique person you are. You did not get to choose your heritage, characteristics, or slot in human history. You do get to choose how you respond.

Does this mean you are complete? Absolutely not, you are a work in progress. God is in the process of perfecting that which concerns us (Psalms 138:8). The New Living Translation reads; "The Lord will work out His plans for my life. . ." He will continue to shape each one of us until we are complete in Him.

God has plans for your life. He designed you and plans to use you in a unique way. What He said to the nation of Israel while they were captive in Babylon can be applied to you and me today. "For I know the plans I have for you, declares the Lord, plans to prosper you and not to harm you, plans to give you hope and a future" (Jeremiah 29:11 NIV).

Life holds tremendous excitement for those who realize that God made them to be something special and that He is in the process of completing what He has begun in them. It is when we bring to the equation the fact that Almighty God is at work in us to give us the desire and the ability to do His good pleasure that life takes on a new and exciting element (Philippians 2:13). It helps us get our focus off of our meager resources and on to the abundance of the Creator of the universe.

Do you know who you are?

Self-Identity Struggle

Chapter II
Biblical Leaders Who Struggled with Self-Identity

Have you concluded that God could never use you to do a mighty work for Him? Have you decided that you are a nobody in the Kingdom of God? It would pay you to listen to the great gospel singer, Ethel Waters, who said "God don't sponsor no junk!" The Bible is full of stories about ordinary people whom God took and made them to be something special.

One of the most helpful facts about the characters God presents to us in the Bible is that He does not airbrush or touch-up the accounts to make them appear uniquely different from ordinary people. Their weaknesses and failures are presented along with the story of God's grace and power in their lives. We learn about them, warts and all.

Several had a problem believing they were capable of doing what God was calling them to do. The ones which we will examine are: Moses, Gideon, Solomon, Jeremiah, and Timothy. Others were scorned by their contemporaries and declared unqualified or unfit to be used of God. Two good examples from this group are David and Saul of Tarsus.

When God got ready to bring His people out of Egypt into the land of promise, He called Moses to lead them. In Exodus 3-4 we have the account of God's call and of the struggle Moses had in answering that call. He used such arguments as: "Who am I to do such a thing?" "They will not believe God sent me" and "I am not a good speaker because I stutter." Yet, God used Moses to accomplish the greatest leadership feat in history. He led approximately 3 million Jews through the desert for forty years.

In Judges 6-8, we have the account of God's call of a man named Gideon to lead Israel in defeating their oppressors, the Midianites. Gideon was hiding when the angel of the Lord called him "a mighty man of valor" and told him that the Lord was with him. Gideon answered by saying, "If the Lord is with us, why are we in this mess?" "Where are the miracles our fathers told us about?" "Why has the Lord left us and delivered us into the hands of the Midianites?" This is not the response of a man of faith or valor. God told Gideon that He was going to use him to deliver Israel from the Midianites.

Gideon's response was "My family is poor and I am the least in my father's house." Gideon had to learn that it was not about him, but about the God he served. God had him diminish his army and fight in a strange way. When he did, God used Gideon to bring great victories to his people.

When Solomon took the throne of his father David, he felt completely inadequate to handle such an awesome task. He told the Lord in I Kings 3 that he was just a child. He admitted he did not know how to go in and out among the people. However, he made a request that touched the heart of God. He asked for wisdom and understanding to lead his people. God made him the wisest man who ever lived apart from Jesus Christ. He became one of the greatest and most loved kings Israel ever had.

When God called Jeremiah to be a prophet to the nation of Israel, God told him that He knew Jeremiah before he was formed in his mother's womb. He had a call on his life before he was ever born. Jeremiah's response was that he did not know how to speak and was only a child. Yet, God put His words in Jeremiah's mouth and made him one of the greatest prophets Israel ever had.

There was a young preacher in the New Testament named Timothy. The Apostle Paul was responsible for bringing him to faith in Christ. He took young Timothy under his wing and began to encourage, challenge and mentor him. We have a record of two letters Paul wrote to Timothy. In them we learn that Timothy was hesitant to speak up because of his youth. He was timid and struggled with fear. Paul admonished him to be strong in the Lord and fight the good fight of faith as a true soldier of the Lord. Wouldn't it be wonderful if all of us had someone like the Apostle Paul to help us become who God intended us to be?

Sometimes we feel that we are not capable of being a useful vessel in the hands of the Lord. We limit our vision by looking at our resources instead of seeing ourselves in the hands of the Lord. Then, there are those of us who are told by people around us that God would never choose to use us. This was certainly true of a young shepherd boy named David. When God told Samuel to go anoint a son of Jesse to be king in the place of Saul, Jesse brought all of his sons before Samuel except David. David was just a youth and he was taking care of the sheep. Apparently, Jesse did not consider David a candidate for the job. However, he was the one chosen by God. When David was sent by his father to take food to his brothers who were battling the Philistines, he asked his brothers why no one was willing to fight the giant Goliath. They made fun of him and told him to go back to keeping the sheep. When David challenged Goliath, the giant laughed and scorned him. David took his slingshot and killed the giant and cut his head off with the giant's own sword. History reveals that David became the greatest king Israel ever had.

Some people are discounted by others because of their past. A good example is Saul of Tarsus. He was such a zealous Jew that he persecuted the early church by having them beaten, imprisoned and even killed. When God called him and changed his life, the church was afraid of him. Barnabas was the one who received him into the fellowship and encouraged others to do as well.

Saul not only experienced a life change, he also had a name change. He became Paul the Apostle to the Gentiles. He admitted that he was the chief of sinners and the least of the apostles. However, no one man did more to advance the kingdom of God on earth than this great man of faith.

In First Corinthians chapter one, Paul discusses the tool box from which God works to accomplish His will on earth. God seldom calls the rich, famous or mighty. He delights in choosing to use someone who would be passed over by a popular vote. He calls a nobody and makes him a somebody so He gets the glory. When you say "I could never do that or be that kind of person," you just moved to the front of the line.

Fellow Struggler

Chapter III

The Confessions of a Fellow Struggler

The conviction with which I state the concepts written in this book is not based on things I have read, but on the thing the Lord has taught me over the years of my journey of faith. Whether we like it or not, much of who we are has been determined by things beyond our control. We must believe that Romans 8:28 is true, especially when it comes to our past. "And we know that all things work together for good to them that love God, to them who are called according to his purpose."

My earliest memories were of the days when we lived on a dairy farm in northeast Mississippi working for someone else. We milked 55 head of cattle twice a day and raised feed crops to see the cattle through the winter. We raised chickens and pigs for our own use and had a large vegetable garden. Dad was what was known as a sharecropper. He was paid $100 per year plus use of a small house without electricity or running water.

Our house was so isolated that we did not merit a regular school bus. There were so few children on our bus route that they sent a pickup truck with a camper on the back to get us. The other kids at school called it the chicken coop. They made fun of us for coming to school in a chicken coop. Children seem to be unaware of the damage done by cruel statements and attitudes.

One year, the owner of the dairy farm told my dad that he was unable to pay him the $100 for the past year. So Dad moved us to the Mississippi Delta where he worked as a mechanic in a factory. To my knowledge, he never made over minimum wage for the rest of his life.

I was the middle child of five children. We never had trademark jeans or designer shirts. Our tennis shoes were the cheapest on the market. We were not able to afford the toys or possessions that many other children had. As a result, my background of poverty caused me to feel inadequate and less than normal.

My parents struggled in their relationship when I was very young. I remember praying night after night that my father and mother would begin to love each other and that our home would be filled with love. There were several forms of abuse that left each of us scarred in our own way. I learned to bury my true feelings deep within so that others would not know the hurt that I carried. I became a loner and spent most of my free time reading novels about happier people in exciting places or roaming through the woods building forts and hunting small game.

When I graduated from high school, I had little ambition with no desire to go to college. I continued to work in a grocery store where I was training to one day be a manager. I probably would still be working in a grocery store if God had not moved in my life in a mighty way.

My life radically changed on January 1, 1963 when I was nineteen years old. My best friend was killed in a hunting accident. I was shaken by the loss of my friend and by the uncertainty of his eternal destination. I realized that I had no guarantee of any certain number of years on this earth. If it had been me, I did not like to think about where I would be.

Although I had been a church member for ten years, I had no change in my lifestyle, inner peace, or assurance of going to heaven when I died. I was raised in church and joined the church with my friends when I was nine years old.

I was saved the next Sunday on January 5, 1963. It is a day I will never forget. The joy and peace that flooded my heart that day has been with me and has carried me for the last fifty years.

After my conversion, I totally surrendered my life to God. I went to work and church and spent the rest of my time studying the Bible, usually into the early hours of the morning. I refused to date for a whole year. I did not want anything to compete with my hunger for the Lord.

Soon after I was saved, God started dealing with me about His plan for my life. I think I went to the altar to pray during every service for almost a year. I knew God wanted me to do something for Him but I was convinced that it was not to preach His Word. I was too bashful to stand before people. There was no way I could become the leader of a church!

Since God would not listen to my excuses, I finally surrendered to preach the Gospel on December 27, 1963. I preached my first sermon four days later. It lasted thirteen minutes. It was a miracle that I could even stand in front of people that long!

My first few attempts to preach were so pitiful that I had the people bowing their heads as I finished. What I wanted to do was run out while they were not looking. I would go home, fall across my bed and weep. I told the Lord that surely He could find someone who could do a better job than what I was doing.

One day He asked me would I be willing to get up and fall flat on my face for Him. I told Him I would. Something changed immediately. It was no longer about me but it was all about Him. I began to think less about how I looked, felt, or sounded and more about what was being said about Him. That was a giant step in my spiritual development.

However, I was a long way from maturity. My personal preference was to be an assistant. I did not like to take the lead. Therefore, when asked to assume a leadership role in some area, I would always volunteer someone else. I would usually say "Why don't you ask John or Bill? Either one can do a much better job than I can."

One day after declining a position of leadership, the Lord smote my heart and told me to never do that again. He told me I was to walk through every door He opened. I made a covenant with the Lord that day. I promised I would walk through every door he opened from that day forward. The agreement included the understanding I would trust Him. He would provide the ability and He would get the credit. The last 25 years have been an exciting journey. He is still working on me but it is amazing the doors He has opened.

I used to believe I had an inferiority complex. One day He showed me that it was not a complex. I was simply inferior! He let me know that without Him I could do nothing (John 15:5). However, He told me at the same time that I can do all things through Christ who strengthens me (Philippians 4:13).

Here is what I have come to believe. I can do anything God wants me to do. The reason is because He is working in me to have the desire and the ability to do what He wants (Philippians 2:13). This is not egotism but faith.

I have come to realize that I am a lousy Billy Graham, but I am the best Ray Gilder God has. I will not have to answer to God for not being a good Billy Graham, but I will have to answer for not being all He wants me to be. There is freedom in being yourself.

The Apostle Paul was right when he said it is unwise to compare ourselves to each other (II Corinthians 10:12). You may be doing better than someone else but he is not your measuring stick. The Lord Jesus Christ is. We really do not need to look at ourselves or each other but to the Lord Jesus Christ, the Author and Finisher of our faith.

Sometime ago I heard someone say that there are three things which can greatly influence who you will be five years from now. They are: the books you read, the friends you make, and how you allow media to influence your thinking. As I thought about that statement, I decided, if that is somewhat true, then I have a lot of control over becoming a better person. First of all, I usually see through the bias presented by the media. My opinions are formed by what God's Word says rather than by what the public thinks or what others want you to think.

Second, I improved and expanded my reading habits. I began adding to my reading list books which challenged me to think outside the box and always ask, "What if?" It is important to not become lazy in my reading and simply read for pleasure, or read only that which agrees with me. We should never be afraid of the truth. It is the truth that sets us free.

Finally, I knew I had to bring new friends into my life. I am a loner by nature and tend to not seek out new friendships. Several years ago, I had a friend who had been a part of my life for over twenty years. In the last few years, this friend had developed a very negative attitude. I could not be in his presence more than a few minutes before he was being critical or negative about most things. As a result, I found myself becoming more and more negative. I did not like who I was becoming.

At the same time, God brought a new friend into my life who inspired me to expand my reading, increased my faith in God and be all that God intended me to be. After being in his presence for a while, I always felt uplifted and encouraged about life and the future. Therefore, I made a conscious decision to back away from the first friendship and cultivate the new friendship. I believe it is one of the most important decisions I have ever made.

We should never conclude: "This is the way I am and I will never be any different." Each one of us is unique but the story of our lives is not complete. We still have several more miles to go before the final chapter is written.

Trying to Please

Chapter IV

The Bondage of Trying to Please Others

One of the most important skills we need to develop as a part of the human race is the ability to relate to the people around us. Social interaction and interpersonal relationships are the source of a lot of unhappiness for many people today. Someone has wittingly stated:

> *To live above with folks with love,*
> *Oh, that would be glory!*
> *To live below with folks we know*
> *Well, that is another story!*

We are expected to love our neighbor, treat him with respect, and seek his well-being. It is commonly agreed that it is wrong to deceive, cheat or hate other people. Relationships often get complicated. In an effort to compensate for one difficult situation, we are often guilty of going overboard in another direction. It would be highly unusual for someone to say "I like for people to hate me!" However, in trying to get people to like us, we may soon find ourselves in the bondage of trying to please other people.

Why Are We Trying To Please Others?

The question needs to be asked, "Why are we trying to please others?" Could it be that you have developed a performance-based sense of self-worth? The only reliable source of your true identity is what the Lord has to say about you. This will be discussed in detail in the next chapter. You are who Christ says you are; not who others say you are. If you are doing what you do to try to get others to think better of you or to approve of you, you will find yourself in constant bondage.

If you suffer from a feeling of inadequacy, you only complicate matters by looking to others to help you feel complete. The truth is: this avenue of resolution will only intensify that feeling. People are fickle. Remember that the same crowd who said about Jesus on Palm Sunday, "Blessed is He who comes in the name of the Lord," said "Crucify him" the next week.

One of the primary motivations for trying to please someone is the fear of their displeasure. To fear displeasing others is to place yourself under the wrong master. Jesus told people that the One we should fear displeasing the most is Almighty God (Matthew 10:28).

Another reason we seek to please others is the desire to fit in. This is especially prevalent among children and youth. However, it is definitely not limited to the younger generation. Loneliness is a universal concern. We need other people. Relationships must be mutually beneficial and based upon respect for each other if they are to be healthy. You can survive without the support and approval of those who do not have your best interest at heart.

The Folly of Trying to Please Others

A lot of well-meaning people out there think they know what you should be doing with your life. There are several problems with that line of thinking. One, they can only see things from their perspective. Two, they filter things through their past experiences, motivation, and goals; not yours. Three, they do not have to live with the consequences, you do.

When you try to please others, you are looking in the wrong direction for instructions on how to live your life. It would be wise for us to remind ourselves frequently that there is only one score card that counts and it is being kept in heaven.

The foolishness of trying to please others is evident when you look at the following realities: they keep changing the rules, and keep raising the bar. It is very discouraging to discover that what they wanted you to do yesterday is not what they want you to do today. Often the person you are trying to please does not really know what he wants. Therefore, you may become a guinea pig for his research. Look at all the things guinea pigs have suffered in order to help mankind find ways to treat certain problems. The life of a guinea pig in a research facility is not the envy of the rodent world. Neither will your friends envy you if your life is controlled by some other person's dictates.

My oldest grandson used to pole vault for the track team at his high school. It takes a lot of training, strength and skill to use the pole to lift your body over the bar. As the competition develops, the bar is raised higher and higher. Eventually, it is raised so high that no one is able to get over it without knocking it down. This is the way some folks will do you if you try to please them. Tomorrow, they will demand more than they did today.

A Key to True Freedom

One of the real paradoxes of this life is the fact that a key to true freedom is to become a servant of Jesus Christ. This is discussed in detail in Romans 6 and other passages throughout the Bible. We are told in John 8 that if the Son of God sets you free, you are free indeed.

It is quite revealing that neither Jesus Christ nor any of his disciples started an anti-slavery movement. While it is not the same, we are comfortable working for someone who controls much of our lives while in their employment. Jesus dealt with the heart where real freedom or bondage is experienced.

Notice what the Apostle Paul said to the slaves, who were members of the church, at Ephesus: "Servants, be obedient to them that are your masters according to the flesh, with fear and trembling, in singleness of your heart, as unto Christ; not with eye-service, as menpleasers; but as the servants of Christ, doing the will of God from the heart; with good will doing service, as to the Lord, and not to men: knowing that whatsoever good thing any man doeth, the same shall he receive of the Lord, whether he be bond or free" (Ephesians 6:5-8, KJV).

He told them not seek to be men pleasers but to please Christ who is their true Master. They were to obey their masters but do it unto Christ who will be their final Judge. Our relationship to Christ is more important than any relationship to other humans. "For he that is called in the Lord, being a servant, is the Lord's freeman: likewise also he that is called, being free, is Christ's servant" (I Corinthians 7:22).

The Call to Please God

While it is apparently counterproductive to try to please others, it is very beneficial to put forth an effort to please God. Paul made it clear that his goal was not to please men but God. "For do I now persuade men, or God? Or do I seek to please men? For if I yet pleased men, I should not be the servant of Christ" (Galatians 1:10).

What would you like to discover and experience: the plans that others have for you, or the plans that God has for you? Here is what Jeremiah told the children of Israel when they were in bondage to Babylon and everything looked extremely bleak. "For I know the plans I have for you, declared the Lord, plans to give you hope and a future" (Jeremiah 29:11, NIV). That statement can be applied as a general principal to God's dealings with His people throughout history.

There are many word pictures used in the Bible to describe a follower of Jesus Christ. One of these is soldier. Paul told Timothy to seek to be a good soldier of Jesus Christ. "Thou therefore endure hardness as a good soldier of Jesus Christ. No man that warreth entangleth himself with the affairs of this life; that he may please him who hath chosen him to be a soldier" (II Timothy 2:3-4). A good soldier does not get involved in things that would hinder him from being ready to obey his commander. We are not to seek to please others but we are to seek to please the One who called us to serve in His army.

Someone may raise the question, "Doesn't the Bible talk about men pleasing their wives and women pleasing their husbands?" Yes, that is discussed in I Corinthians 7. However, the emphasis is made that pleasing God is a priority. We should seek to be the best mate we can be. We should have the interests of our mates at heart. However, the truth is that when we are what God wants us to be, we become a better husband, wife, father, mother, son, daughter, friend or neighbor.

In order to please God, we must learn to trust Him because the Bible teaches "without faith it is impossible to please Him" (Hebrews 11:6). This means to come to the conclusion that God knows what is best. God is doing what is best for you and God will bring to a proper conclusion what He has started.

A verse in the Book of Proverbs that has been one of my life verses is Proverbs 16:7: "When a man's ways please the Lord, he maketh even his enemies to be at peace with him." When I focus on pleasing God, my life is much more successful and pleasant than when I focus on pleasing others.

When our Lord was on this earth, God spoke from heaven and said, "This is my beloved Son in whom I am well pleased." Do you think it might be possible for God to say the same thing about us? One of our goals should be to hear Him say when this life is over, "Well done, thy good and faithful servant."

True Identity

Chapter V
The One Source of Your True Identity

Only God knows who you really are. The Bible is clear that you can be deceived by Satan, by others, and even by yourself. Before we look at who God says you are, let us examine several sources of false identity.

Sources of False Identity

The Good or Bad Deeds You Have Done in the Past

All of us are ashamed of some bad things we have done in the past. Also, most of us are proud of a few good things we have done. Neither of these individual actions define our true identity. It is only as these actions become a habitual pattern do they become a part of our identity.

Some people make a big mistake and do something they regret. As a result, they come to believe they will never amount to anything because of what they have done. Many people struggle with the ability to forgive themselves. It is wonderful to know that when God forgives, He forgets! While we may not be able to forget what we have confessed to God, we must learn to stamp "Paid in full!" over that memory.

Pride is a great enemy of true identity. I heard a story years ago about a woodpecker who traveled into the Petrified Forest in Arizona. Just as he was about to peck on one of those stone-like trees, a lightning bolt struck the tree. The tree split in half and fell to the ground. It is reported that during the next six months, this proud woodpecker led delegations of woodpeckers to the site and boasted loudly, "Right over here is where I did it!" Just like that woodpecker, we have the tendency to take credit for many things we think we accomplished without the help of God or others.

A Reputation You Have Developed Over Time

The root meaning of reputation is "public opinion." Public opinion is formed by what others say about an individual, how that individual is portrayed in the news media, and how this individual performs in the public arena. How often have fans become disappointed when they have a face to face encounter with their hero. If you have a reputation, you are motivated to live up to it even though you may feel like a hypocrite. I am convinced that transparency is a great trait to possess.

The Apostle Paul was quite transparent when he stated in I Corinthians 15:10, "But by the grace of God I am what I am. . ." The secret is to just be who you are.

A Curse Placed on You by Others

Holman Illustrated Bible Dictionary states that "blessing" and "cursing" are key biblical emphases, as reflected by 544 uses of various forms of the word "bless" and 282 occurrences of various forms of the word "curse" in the ESV. (Holman Illustrated Bible Dictionary; Trent Butler, ed.; Nashville: Holman Bible Publishers; 1998; pp.223-4). While receiving a blessing is a very positive experience, receiving a curse is not. The editors of the Holman Illustrated Bible Dictionary define receiving a "curse" in this way: "Depending on who is speaking, one who 'curses' is either predicting, wishing or praying for, or causing great trouble on someone, or he is calling for an object to be a source of such trouble" (pg. 224). The curse that is placed on many people today comes from family members or significant persons of influence in an individual's life. Here are a couple of examples of that kind of curse: "He will never amount to anything." And "He will always be a loser." No matter what anyone has said about you in the past, you can become all that God wants you to be.

Family Tradition

Families tend to develop certain names in a community based on what previous members of that family have done. It is true that we often bear some resemblance to our parents and grandparents. However, we do not have to follow their ways and imitate their traits. God created us with a will. We can choose to be different. We can choose to be like Christ. You do not have to do what your family has always done or become what your father or grandfather has been. We have all known two siblings who were completely opposite in temperament and behavior. You may be the one to break the negative pattern in your family.

The Person Someone Wants You to Be

Is someone trying to control your life? It could be a mother, father, friend, or teacher. Some parents try to relive their lives through their children. Many children are challenged to become something they are not in order to please their parents. When some young children participate in sports programs, it is not the desire of the child but the surrogate wishes of the parents. This is often followed in later life by the parents trying to choose the profession of their children. Parents should be commended when they encourage and challenge their children. However, the attempt to control the future of their children should be discouraged. You will answer to God for who you become, not your parents.

The Person You Have Decided to Copy

Without a doubt, Elvis Presley was one of the most gifted singers this world has ever known. His stage appearance was so unique that hundreds if not thousands of impersonators have tried to dress, sing, and act like Elvis Presley. I have a cousin who was recognized as one of the top twenty-five Elvis impersonators in the world. As a result, he was invited to Nashville to perform at the Ryman Auditorium. While he may be pretty good at being like Elvis, watching him will present few clues as to his true identity. Who do you want to be like? While we should seek to develop the positive qualities of other people, we must learn to be ourselves.

The Person Satan Says You Are

One of the titles given to Satan in the Bible is "The Accuser of the brethren" (Revelation 12:10). It needs to be recognized that he is good at what he does. He accuses us to God, to others, and to ourselves. One of his chief weapons is to tell someone that because he has done some specific sin "God does not love you anymore." And "God cannot use you." Here are some of his favorite tools: doubt, depression, discouragement, lies, slander, rumors, fear, and physical attacks. It actually comes down to who do you really believe: your Father who loves you or the enemy of your soul, Satan?

The Person You Feel Like at the Moment

While most of us will agree that you cannot trust your feelings at the moment to determine your future status, too often many folks trust their current feelings to indicate their standing before God. To be honest, there are times when I do not feel saved, have a desire to keep on living, believe that my future will ever get any better, or that God even hears my prayers. A key concept in Christian development is to understand that growth comes in this sequence: Fact-Faith-Feeling. The Apostle Paul demonstrated this when he was on a ship headed for Rome and it was overtaken by a great storm. The sailors did everything they knew to save the ship from destruction, but to no avail. The Bible says "all hope that we should be saved was taken away" (Acts 27:20). An angel appeared to Paul and told him they would be spared. Here is the statement we need to repeat: "Wherefore, sirs, be of good cheer: for I believe God. . ." (Acts 27:25).

The Source of Your True Identity

After looking at several sources of false identity, let's turn to God and His Word to learn what He has to say about who we are. The Psalmist was captured by his understanding of God's special work in making him who he was. Listen to how he describes his unique development: "You alone created my inner being. You knitted me together inside my mother. I will give thanks to you because

I have been so amazingly and miraculously made. Your works are miraculous, and my soul is fully aware of this. My bones were not hidden from you when I was being made in secret, when I was being skillfully woven in an underground workshop. Your eyes saw me when I was only a fetus. Every day of my life was recorded in your book before one of them had taken place. How precious are your thoughts concerning me, O God! How vast in number they are! If I try to count them, there would be more of them than there are grains of sand. When I wake up, I am still with you" (Psalms 139:13-18, God's Word Translation).

Every one of God's creatures are of infinite value. Never confuse your disappointment over your sinful nature with your worth as a person. The text above indicates the value God has placed upon you. This should lead you to discover the joy and freedom of being yourself. From this text, several things should grab your attention.

God Personally Put You Together in Your Mother's Womb

God put the right combination of genes together to make you one-of-a-kind. The Psalmist said that God "knit him together." "Curiously wrought" means "wrought with care." It literally means "woven or embroidered with threads of different colors." God made only one of you. The world will never see another person exactly like you. God's originals are all masterpieces and can never be duplicated.

What you do not like about yourself is a criticism of God's creative design. The Psalmist said he was fearfully and wonderfully made.

God Knew All About You Before You were Born

Nothing about you ever surprises God. His eyes have been upon you since before you were born. He has loved you before you were born. Do not try to impress God like you do others. You try to impress others and hope that they do not see you in your bad moments. God knows all about them and still loves you.

God Ordered Your Days in Advance

The King James Version translation says "all my members" but it should be "all my days." Nothing that has happened to you has surprised God. He planned it. God designed your personality, your appearance and your experiences to make you the special person He wants you to be. You are where you are today because God is doing His special work in your life. It would pay you to try to find out what God is doing and agree with what He is doing and cooperate with Him.

God's Thoughts are on You at All Times

God's thoughts toward you are beyond number. The Psalmist said that if he tried to count God's thoughts about him they would be more than there are grains of sand. David said that if he "would declare and speak of them, they are more than can be numbered" (Psalms 40:5). His thoughts toward you are thoughts of peace and for a purpose as God told Israel in Jeremiah 29:11.

God's Presence is With You Continually

God's presence is with you whether you are awake or asleep. In verses 8-12 of Psalm 139, the Psalmist said that he could never go any place where God is not present. He also stated that it did not matter whether it was day or night. God sees just as well in the darkness as in the light. Instead of this bringing fear, it should be a source of great comfort to those who love God and want to please Him.

Your true identity is who God says you are and who He knows you to be. God made you. God knows you. God loves you. Do you praise Him for making you like you are? Do you honor Him by being yourself and by using your special personality to glorify God?

New Birth

Chapter VI
The Importance of the New Birth

One of the possible responses to the title of this book, *The Freedom of Being Yourself,* is to conclude that it contains New-Age concepts. I was aware of that possibility when I chose the title. However, just a casual reading of a few pages should negate that line of reasoning. I am not encouraging folks to develop some spark of inner divine being. I am challenging them to view themselves through the eyes and words of their Creator. I am not suggesting self-hate or self-love but self-realization so one can become confident to say with the Psalmist, "I am fearfully and wonderfully made" (Psalms 139:14). However, to be able to say with the Apostle Paul, "But by the grace of God I am what I am. . ." (I Corinthians 15:10), one must become the recipient of the grace of God which comes as a result of a second birth or being born again. Only the Bible can provide clear insight into the importance of a second birth.

God's Original Design

As we view the world in which we live today, we need to realize that this is not what God had originally designed. We have to go to the book of Genesis to discover the beauty and harmony of the original creation. Every time God made something new, He looked at it and said, "It was good." As God put the finishing touches on His creation by making man, He looked at what He had made and said, "It was very good."

Adam and Eve lived in a perfect world in total innocence, complete holiness, and simple freedom. They enjoyed unbroken fellowship with each other and with God. God gave them everything they needed to experience life at its best. Nothing was denied them except the fruit of one of the trees in the midst of the Garden of Eden, the tree of the knowledge of good and evil. God warned them that if they ate that fruit, they would die.

The Action That Warped the Design

Through the influence of the Serpent, they chose to disobey God and ate the forbidden fruit. While they did not fall over dead physically, they died spiritually and became aware of what it is like to know evil. They began to experience things they had never experienced before. They learned what it is like to feel guilt. They learned what it is like to be afraid. They lost their innocence and became aware of their nakedness. They wanted to hide from God and they learned to blame someone else for their actions.

That day became the darkest day in human history. God's original design became warped by sin. The descendants of Adam and Eve became sinners by nature and by choice. The earth was given a curse. Nothing has been the same since.

The Hopelessness of Repairing the Design

Mankind lost something on that dreadful day in the Garden of Eden that he has been trying to repair or replace ever since. It is not within the power of man to fix himself. Man has tried to correct the situation through various approaches. Some try to deny that a problem exists. They believe they are fine without God. Others try to pretend that things are better than they really are deep inside their hearts. Then, there are those who work extra hard to earn favor with God. None of these efforts produce peace in the heart of man or acceptance in the presence of God.

The Possibility of a New Design

God knew from the beginning that man would face this dilemma. God designed a plan to offer a new life to fallen man. He sent His Son, Jesus Christ, to pay for man's sin and provide a new start through faith in Christ. That is why the Apostle Paul could say, "If any man be in Christ, he is a new Creation: old things are passed away, behold, all things are become new" (II Corinthians 5:17). When a person is born again, his outward features do not change but he is given a new heart and spirit. He soon realizes he is not the man he used to be. He now has a heart after God.

The Potential of the New Design

When God gives a person new life, the potential of that life is based upon the power of God and not the heritage or resources of that individual. That is why Paul could say without being proud or boastful, "I can do all things through Christ who strengthens me" (Philippians 4:13). We are told by the Lord Jesus Christ that nothing shall be impossible to him who believes (Matthew 17:20). This may be hard for some folks to comprehend but a believer in Christ can do everything God wants him to do if he is willing to trust Christ to give him the ability. The words "I can't" should be dropped from the vocabulary of every Christian. If God wants him to do something; he can with the help of God. If God does not want him to do something, he should not try it. The sad truth about most Christians is that they never reach their full potential.

The Uniqueness of the New Design

The unique design of each child of God is the basic premise of this book. Every person has a God-given design that is unique to them. At the new birth a person receives spiritual gifts and abilities which are to be developed in order for that person to fulfill his place in God's history. Success in this life is discovering God's plan for your life and fulfilling that plan to the best of your ability. This is why trying to copy others is a poor way to live one's life on this earth.

The Responsibility for Design Change

Every person born into this world is a descendant of a fallen human race. God has provided a way to receive a new life through faith in His Son, Jesus Christ. When a person hears the good news of the Gospel, he is given a choice. He can remain in a spiritually dead state or he can receive new life through Christ. That is a decision which cannot be handed to anyone else. It is the responsibility of the followers of Christ to share the Gospel with every person on the face of the earth. The choice of receiving a design change is the responsibility of every person who hears the Gospel.

Whether or not to be born again is the single most important decision a person will make while living on this earth. The greatest results of being born again is the knowledge and assurance that you will live forever in a wonderful place called heaven. The second great benefit is the potential to live life on earth to the highest level possible. One thing is certain, you can never experience all that you could be without the new birth.

Not Wanting To Be

Chapter VII

Reasons for not wanting to be Yourself

Few people are as comfortable with who they are as one of my favorite cartoon characters from when I was growing up. His name was "Popeye." He was always going around singing, "I am what I am and that is all that I am. I am Popeye the sailor man." When a person refuses to be himself, he ends up playing a part like an actor in the theater. Jesus Christ accused the religious leaders in His day of being "hypocrites," which is the word for an actor in a play. I am convinced that Jesus would classify most folks today as "hypocrites" because they are not who they want others to think they are. This leads to a sobering question, "Why do people not want to be themselves?" Let's examine some possibilities.

A Poor Self-Image

A lot of people have grown up not liking themselves. This attitude can be developed from several sources. Some experience excessive criticism as a child. It could have come from a perfectionist parent or playmates at school who delight in picking on others to keep the attention off of themselves. Some child may have said to a classmate, "You smell bad!" This could lead to a compulsion about odor which drives the victim to applying deodorant several times a day for the rest of his life. Many teenagers are constantly struggling over some aspect of their bodies which make them feel uncomfortable. People with a poor self-image limit their accomplishments as adults because they never allow themselves the freedom to be who God made them. There are two things I would like to say to those who have a poor self-image. First of all, most people never notice the small imperfections with which you are obsessed. Second, those who know you have a better opinion of you than you do about yourself.

A Feeling of Inadequacy

No one ever learned to walk the first time they tried. That is why parents will applaud every step their child takes and pick him up when he falls and say, "You can do it! You can do it!" We all know that the key is to keep trying. This is true about almost everything in life. The problem for many people is that there was no one available to pick them up at critical times in their lives.

It must be agreed that no one is an expert in every area of life. However, all of us have special gifts and abilities. While you may not be good at one thing, you may be better than average at something else. Nevertheless, even those labeled "natural-born athletes" must exercise, train and work hard to reach their full potential. One of the key traits of a good leader is to recognize the potential in people. Then, they must be given an opportunity to receive training, to perform on the field, and to be coached through the learning process.

A False Concept of the Humanity of Others

Why do we often feel that someone else can do a better job than we can? It is a natural tendency to feel that other people do not struggle with most of the things which give us trouble. It is interesting to note that when a group of people get honest with each other, they find that most of them struggle with the same issues.

Why do you often feel that the life others around you live is so much simpler and easier than the life you live? The truth is, everybody around you has feet of clay. They probably think you have it made. All of us have our own version of the old spiritual song, "Nobody knows the trouble I've seen; nobody knows my cradle of sorrow."

Peter gives us insight into the common problems faced by most followers of Christ when he said, "knowing that the same afflictions are accomplished in your brethren that are in the world" (I Peter 5:9). Other people have lived through what you are facing and have finished well. As has been stated before, it is neither wise nor profitable to compare yourself to other people.

A Desire to be Someone You Are Not

It is one thing to want to be like another person. It is quite different to want to be that person. All Christians are called to model their lives after Christ. However, pity the man who thinks he is Christ. The Apostle Paul challenged his readers to follow him as he followed Christ (I Thessalonians 1:6).

It would be interesting to know how many young preachers have sought to sound like and act like Billy Graham. Billy Graham ran his race well and finished his assignment, but you have to run your own race. Every one of us will have to answer to God for what we did with what He gave us.

Years ago, I jokingly said that I was tempted to send the picture of a famous movie star when asked for a picture to be used to promote some event where I was speaking. When that movie star died, his secret life of moral failure was made public. After all was said and done, I was especially glad I had never used his picture to portray me. I was glad to be myself instead of being like him.

A Refusal to Die to Self

A root problem which haunts all of mankind is pride. We often desire for others to think better of us than they should. When we accept ourselves as God made us, we can live in the reality of who we are without wanting to impress others through our pretense.

Humility is a virtue which is championed throughout the Bible. It is when we think more of ourselves than we should, that we end up embarrassed when the reality becomes evident. King Saul of Israel lost his kingdom because he tried to be something he was not, a priest. He got tired of waiting on Samuel and offered the sacrifice himself. Here is what Samuel said to him: "And Samuel said, When thou wast little in thine own sight, wast thou not made the head of the tribes of Israel, and the Lord anointed thee king over Israel?" (I Samuel 15:17).

As one matures in his walk with God, he discovers that life is really not about him but about Jesus Christ. Self-esteem, pride and poor self-image must be eliminated as we find our place in God's plan to bring glory and honor to our Creator.

Marred Vessels

Chapter VIII
What God Does With Marred Vessels

Too many Christians are not living up to their calling as children of God. The most frequently used excuse is the statement, "But you do not know what has happened to me." It would certainly be wrong to minimize the difficult experiences some folks have had to face. Unless we have been through the exact same set of circumstances, we cannot fully know how those things would affect us. However, as children of God, we have the assurance that our Father in heaven is at work to accomplish His purposes through our lives.

As we look around us today, we see many whose lives have been traumatized by disappointments, heartaches and defeat. Many of them are not nearly the person they used to be. An honest assessment would classify these individuals as marred vessels.

There is wonderful news for these folks. God specializes in remaking marred vessels. This truth was demonstrated to the Prophet Jeremiah as God revealed to him what He was doing to the nation Israel. "The word which came to Jeremiah from the Lord, saying, arise and go down to the potter's house, and there I will cause thee to hear my words. Then I went down to the potter's house, and, behold, he wrought a work on the wheels. And the vessel that he made of clay was marred in the hand of the potter: so he made it again another vessel, as seemed good to the potter to make it" (Jeremiah 18:1-4).

The Potter's Design

God is the potter and we are the clay. When the potter places the clay on the wheel, he has a design in mind for that lump of clay. God is in the process of making vessels that please Him. It is our responsibility to allow Him to shape us into the vessel He desires. Paul shared this truth with Timothy in II Timothy 2:21: "If a man therefore purge himself from these, he shall be a vessel unto honour, sanctified, and meet for the master's use, and prepared unto every good work."

The vessel God makes is a vessel to honor. To honor what or whom? Not the vessel but the Potter. All of us are original creations of God. We are to honor our Creator.

It is also a sanctified vessel. This means it is set apart for God's use. Christians are not to be like other people. They are the vessels of a holy God.

The vessel is intended to be used to accomplish a good work. Every child of God should ask himself the question, "What has God designed me to accomplish in my service to Him?'

The Potter's Disappointment

As Jeremiah watched, the vessel became marred in the potter's hand. The potter is disappointed over what the clay has become. Who knows exactly what happened to cause the vessel to become marred? Every marred vessel has its own story.

There are a lot of people today who could be classified as marred vessels. Has something happened to you that has kept you from becoming what God intended you to be? Has someone you had confidence in let you down? Has a number of bad things happened to you that keeps knocking you down when you try to get back up?

A marred vessel does not bring honor to God. A marred vessel is of no use to God. Can you say that God is pleased with your life today?

The Potter's Determination

One of the most wonderful things about the Divine Potter is that He does not throw away the marred vessel. As Jeremiah watched, the potter remade the clay into another vessel. If we were to ask the clay, "Does it hurt to be mashed down and reshaped?" I am sure it would say "yes." However, the Potter knows what He is doing.

This is one of the reasons we should never give up on some brother who has stumbled. We must help restore him to the place where God can reshape him. There may come a time when we will need his help to get back up.

Before his untimely death, our son, Stephen, gave my wife and me one of the most cherished gifts we have ever received. While they were riding together, he said to his mother, "I really love you and dad. I feel I have the best parents in the world. I know that no matter what I do, you are not going to throw me away!" There were times he tried our patience but we never left a doubt regarding our love for him and our commitment to his well-being.

If you have become a marred vessel, the best thing you can do is get back on the potter's wheel. Place your life back into the hands of God. There is a danger of becoming so hardened that you can no longer be reshaped.

The Potter's Delight

As the potter continued reshaping the marred vessel, he ended up making it into another vessel that seemed good to him. God delights in taking a marred vessel and reworking it into something very special. It may not be what it used to be but the Master Designer can make it into something even better. You may have failed God in one area and are no longer useful in that area but God can reshape you to serve in another area. The fact that you are still here is an indication that God is not through using you.

The words of the great song writer, Bill Gaither, is the testimony of many marred vessels which have been reshaped by God.

"Something beautiful, something good

All my confusion He understood.

All I had to offer Him was brokenness and strife

But He made something beautiful of my life."

The Importance

Chapter IX
The Importance of Being Yourself

A statement which is frequently made by someone who has a bad self-image is "I hate myself!" This is often made by a young teenager who is struggling with the awkwardness of adjusting to an ever-changing body and emotional state. It becomes very tempting to look at others who seem to have it all together and wish to trade places with them. On several occasions, I have discovered that the other person felt the same about the one who was envying him. A great secret about contentment in this life is to learn to just be yourself.

God is the Master Designer. He knew what He was doing when He designed you for a special place in His master plan. We need to acknowledge God's ability to put the plans together just like we do when we hire an architect to draw the plans for a building. The average person can tell very little about the drawings. However, the builder can take them and produce the desired product. This is what the Apostle Paul meant when he said, "From whom the whole body fitly joined together and compacted by that which every joint supplieth according to the effectual working in the measure of every part, maketh increase of the body unto the edifying of itself in love" (Ephesians 4:16). Simply stated, every part of the body of Christ must find its place and do its part for the body to grow.

As we examine the importance of being yourself, we must begin with the understanding that God made you like He wanted you and that He has a purpose for your existence. Several reasonable conclusions can be reached from that understanding. While these statements are self-evident, they can drive home the importance of being yourself.

If you do not want to be yourself, you are insulting your Maker

If you were in a museum that featured paintings by Rembrandt and van Gogh and you began to make fun of each painting, what would that prove? It would not discredit those famous artists but would indicate that you do not appreciate fine art. If you found an original painting by one of these men in an attic of an old house you just bought, what would you do? You would probably dust it off, seek to restore the framing to its original state and then hang it in a prominent place in your home. The value of the piece of canvas is not the issue. It is what the master did to it. God designed you for a purpose. Do not insult Him by criticizing His design. Every child of God is, ". . . his workmanship, created in Christ Jesus unto good works. . ." (Ephesians 2:10).

If you are not yourself, the best you can be is second best

Have you discovered that original prints are much more valuable than copies of the same painting? Would you be willing to trade an original for a copy of another original? Yet, that is what we do when we try to copy someone else. As I stated earlier, I am a lousy Billy Graham but I am the best Ray Gilder God has. The secret is to discover who God made you to be. Underneath the dust of neglect and misuse is an original which God wants to put on display in His Kingdom to demonstrate to the world His grace and unique ability. We are not in competition with those around us. Each of us has a special place in the Master Plan. Do not seek or settle for the opportunity to be a copy of someone else. By the way, God is the Master Appraiser who determines the value of each of His creations. To settle for the evaluation of some other person is to rely on an unqualified judge.

You are the best YOU there is or ever will be

Have you noticed that there are a lot of people on the earth? Do you find yourself feeling insignificant? In every arena of life, we are identified by a number. That causes us to feel less than important. However, God knows your name, He knows where you are, He knows what you have done and are doing and He even knows what you are thinking. Does that not make you feel a little more significant? Your story is being written every day. Your story will be shared in eternity. Are you interested in your story being complete with a happy ending? Then, I suggest you get busy allowing God to make you into what He wants. Decide that you are going to be all God wants you to be by His grace and through the power of the Holy Spirit. There will never be another you. Do not miss the opportunity to glorify your Creator.

No one can speak from your experience but you

There is a missing ingredient in many worship services today: people do not share with the congregation what God has done for them in the past week. Many times after a service, someone has come up to me to tell how God met a special need or answered a specific prayer. My response is usually to say that this story should have been shared with the entire congregation. This is what David talked about in Psalm 40: "I have not hid thy righteousness within my heart; I have declared thy faithfulness and thy salvation: I have not concealed thy lovingkindness and thy truth from the great congregation" (Psalms 40:10). No one can tell your story like you can. It is good to hear from someone how God blessed their friend. It is much better to hear the story first-hand. Remember what our Lord said, ". . . if these should hold their peace, the stones would immediately cry out" (Luke 19:40). Every Christian is a trophy of God's grace. We were made to praise the Lord. When we tell our story, others are encouraged to trust the Lord as well. Listen to David's story and the results of his sharing, "I waited patiently for the Lord; and he inclined unto me, and heard my cry. He brought me up also out of an horrible pit, out of the miry clay, and set my feet upon a rock, and established my goings. And he hath put a new song in my mouth, even praise unto our God: many shall see it, and fear, and shall trust in the Lord" (Psalm 40:1-3). Your story needs to be told by you. Do not rob God of praise or yourself of a blessing by failing to tell others what God has done in your life.

You do not have to remember a part

If you are not being yourself then you are copying someone else, which means you must remember a part and not do just what comes naturally. I have often been amazed at the change in speech and voice tone many preachers adopt when they enter the pulpit to deliver a message. Instead of speaking in his normal tone, a preacher may often speak much slower and with a much deeper voice as if to appear more reverent. There is nothing wrong with raising the voice at times to make a point but it needs to come through the personality of the speaker and not as a poor imitation of some famous preacher. Sometimes you will hear a preacher speak with a special accent and later forget to use the same accent when saying the same word. Preachers with a distinguished accent attract the attention of those from other areas where that accent is not common. Poor imitations are not that appealing. Be yourself. There is no one just like you.

Only you can decide what God has planned for you

It is quite interesting to learn that many folks have a strong opinion about what you should do with your life. I have had some folks tell me what God's will for my life was. It is good to know that others are so interested in you and your future to want to have input. However, when God wants to tell someone what he needs to do, He tells that person, not someone else. No one else will have to answer to God for what you do or not do with your life. The temptation is to sell yourself short by looking at yourself instead of to God. Every one of us is a masterpiece in the making. What is required is a close and personal relationship with the Father. Too often we decide within our own mind what would be best. Then, we spend a lot of time begging God to bless what we have chosen. Also, we spend too much time looking at other models. Faith requires being a risk taker. However, it is not really a risk if you are being led by the Holy Spirit. The true risk is trying to plan your life on your own. Learn to be yourself by discovering and developing into all God wants you to be.

The Possibilities

Chapter X
The Possibilities from Being Yourself

Do you realize that there has never been anyone just like you before and there will never be anyone just like you after you are gone? You have a golden opportunity to be somebody, so do not mess it up! You have the potential to bring much glory to God. This can only happen as you are "filled with all the fullness of God" (Ephesians 3:19). Remember, you are just the vessel. The world has yet to see a man who is completely full of God.

We limit what God can do in and through us by our small imagination. When the Apostle Paul prayed for the Christians at Ephesus, he realized that the potential rested in "him that is able to do exceedingly abundantly above all that we ask or think, according to the power that worketh in us,. . ." (Ephesians 3:20). Truly the possibilities of what can happen when we learn to be who God made us are limited only by the extent of our faith and obedience. Learning to be yourself frees you to:

Dream

Dreams come in two forms. The first is the dream which we have while we are sleeping. We have almost no control over these kinds of dreams, be they good dreams or bad dreams. Watching what you eat just before you go to bed may help. The second kind of dream is to meditate in your mind concerning how things could be. Our mind is a wonderful gift from God. With our minds we can remember things in the past, reason out a logical conclusion, determine to act in a certain way, choose right or wrong, and plan a preferred future.

How much time do you spend dreaming about what God may want to do through you? A question you should ask yourself on a regular basis is "what if?" When we remember that we can join the Apostle Paul in saying, "I can do all things through Christ who strengtheneth me" (Philippians 4:13), the possibilities are endless. A biblical term for this kind of dreaming is meditation. Meditation allows the Spirit of God to plant seed-thoughts in your mind which may germinate and produce results you never thought possible. That is what Paul said to the Philippian believers; "For it is God which worketh in you both to will and to do of his good pleasure" (Philippians 2:13). In laymen's terms this just means that God gives us the desire and the ability to do what He wants. Being yourself allows you to dream big.

Develop

All of us are born with certain talents and abilities. Some folks have a talent for singing, playing basketball, or building things with their hands. I have always had a great desire to sing songs of praise to God. However, one of my church deacons helped me face reality one day when he said, "I cannot sing either but I do not cry about it!" Singing lessons will not help me. Therefore, I look forward to getting a new voice in heaven. My youngest brother on the other hand was born with a wonderful voice. I loved to hear him sing. I do not think he used his voice enough while on this earth. I firmly believe he is singing his heart out in the presence of the Lord today.

People with talents and abilities must develop them to bring about the best results. The greatest of the talented athletes must still work hard to develop the talents they were given at birth. Have you noticed that the offspring of talented people often end up doing the same thing their parents did and sometimes even better? This indicated inherited ability.

Being yourself means to learn to develop all that God put in your genes at birth. All those abilities have been given to you for a purpose. What is it that comes easy for you? What do you have a natural tendency to do? It is a waste of God's investment if you do not work to develop what you have.

Discover

When a person is born physically, he is born with certain natural talents and abilities. When a person is born spiritually, he is born with certain gifts and abilities which are given by the Spirit of God. These are spiritual gifts or gifts of grace. Every child of God has at least one and probably more spiritual gifts given by the Holy Spirit at the time of conversion. Paul made this statement as he began discussing spiritual gifts in the book of Romans, "God in his kindness gave each of us different gifts. . ." (Romans 12:6, God's Word Translation). Then, Paul lists and describes seven motivational gifts. As you seek to be yourself, you need to discover which motivational gift God has given you by His Spirit. It is as we operate through our motivational gift that we find our greatest freedom and fulfillment. Time will not permit a detailed study of spiritual gifts but every child of God should seek to discover how God has gifted him so he can be of the most benefit to the body of Christ.

A brief testimony may prove beneficial. I was saved and called to preach under the ministry of a pastor whose motivational gift was prophecy. He was very strong in pronouncing judgment on much that folks in the congregation were doing. When I started preaching, I tried to copy the style of preaching that my pastor used. I soon discovered that I had to be me. After studying spiritual gifts, I discovered that my motivational gift was mercy. My style of preaching is with a broken heart over sin, not harsh statements. Both of us feel the same about sin and disobedience. However, our ministry style is based on our spiritual gift.

Depend on God

Faith plays a very important role in becoming who God made you to be. One of the greatest statements of faith recorded in the Bible is found in the book of Philippians, "I can do all things through Christ which strengtheneth me" (Philippians 4:13). God likes for His children to claim His promises and to trust Him to work through them. The question is not how big are you but how big is your God? If God leads you to do something, He will supply the resources. God never leaves a job half done. Listen to what Paul said, "Being confident of this very thing, that he which hath begun a good work in you will perform it until the day of Jesus Christ" (Philippians 1:6). What He has started in us will not stop until we stand complete before our Savior in heaven. Trusting God should not be our last resort but our first response. If Jesus were to say unto you "Be it unto you according to your faith," what would you become? As the missionary of old, William Carey, said; "Expect great things from God. Attempt great things for God."

Dare to be Different

Nobody should set out to be an odd-ball. Neither should we set as a goal to become like everybody else. We should accept the fact that we are unique. Many who have exceptional abilities tend to hide them, especially children, because we want to be accepted and become like those around us. We are all different in one way or another. It is God who made us "to differ from another" (I Corinthians 4:7). Therefore, we must not stifle the creative genius of our God. Have you ever thought about becoming the first _____? You can fill in the blank. To become the first at anything, you will probably fail at several other endeavors. Even in the area you finally become the first, you will undoubtedly fail many times before you get it right. To dare to be different requires courage. Are you willing to take a dare? I dare you to trust God and be willing to be everything He wants you to be!

Delight the Heart of God

All parents are delighted when their children do those things which please them. Our Father in heaven is watching His children today with a careful eye. Are you touched by the fact that you have the potential to delight your God? We know this is possible because He expressed His pleasure in His Son Jesus Christ on several occasions. "This is my beloved Son in who I am well pleased" (Matthew 3:17, 17:5, II Peter 1:17).

How many fathers have cheered their children as they performed in an athletic event by saying when it was over, "I knew you could do it!"? Your biggest Cheerleader is your Father in heaven. He wants to see you give Him your best and do what He designed you to do. What sweet words await those who finish their course and land in heaven just in time to hear "Well done thou good and faithful servant!"

The Journey

Chapter XI
The Journey to Becoming All You Can Be

When does a person become a human being? Some would say at birth, but I would say at conception. The potential for your development was present when you were conceived. However, your appearance at conception or at birth was nothing compared to what you look like today. It may surprise you to know that there is still much potential in you that has yet to be realized or developed. Many a parent has grieved when they discover that their child's mind, motor skills, or social abilities stopped developing at a young age.

How do you think your Father in heaven feels about your spiritual development? God is interested in every aspect of your life reaching its full potential. This was voiced by the Apostle Paul when he said, "And the very God of peace sanctify you wholly; and I pray God your whole spirit and soul and body be preserved blameless unto the coming of our Lord Jesus Christ" (I Thessalonians 5:23). Several factors are involved in the process of you becoming all you can be. Below is a list of some of the more important ones.

Come Alive to God by a Spiritual Birth

As has been mentioned in detail in chapter VI, you were designed to be alive unto God spiritually as well as physically. The earlier that spiritual birth takes place the better. We must grow spiritually as we grow physically. Some people wait until later in life before deciding to respond to the Gospel. No matter how talented or committed to a cause a person may be, he will never reach his full potential without life from above. Most people will say that they did not begin to really live until they were born again. Everyone can use a guide as they make the decisions which impact the rest of their lives. The Holy Spirit comes to live in you the moment you are saved. As you choose to walk in the Spirit and not in the flesh, your life takes on a new dynamic. The Word of God takes on new meaning. You now have a Guidebook that is completely trustworthy.

Accept Your Identity with Humility and Grace

Are you comfortable with who you are? You should never think you are better than someone else. Neither should you think that you are not as good as other folks. Your worth is based on the fact that God made you. You are not a "self-made man." You may have worked hard at what you do. You may work harder than most around you. However, all you have done is develop the "you" God made. Humility is championed as one of the most valued virtues in the Bible. It does not indicate weakness but strength under control. Paul used these words to describe this point, "But by the grace of God I am what I am: and his grace which was bestowed upon me was not in vain; but I labored more abundantly than they all: yet not I, but the grace of God which was with me" (I Corinthians 15:10). As recipients of grace, we do not have reason to exalt ourselves. However, we are to use our lives to exalt the One who made us and called us to follow Him.

Study the Word of God

As I mentioned earlier, the Word of God is your Guidebook. It is our manual for life. The Word of God must become your daily food if you are to grow spiritually. The wisdom found in the Word of God should provide guidance for every decision you make. Secure as many study helps as you can find. One good thought is worth the price of a book. The more you get into the Word of God, the more it gets into you. Have you noticed that the content of the Bible has never been updated? The different translations are for our benefit to help us see clearly what God has been saying all along. As promised Joshua, if we follow His commandments, He will make our way prosperous and we will have good success (Joshua 1:7-8).

Become a Person of Faith

Faith in God is the key to living an extraordinary life. Real faith relies on the resources of God and not what the individual can do. My favorite chapter in the Bible is Philippians 4. I call it the "Positive Christianity" chapter. I find myself going to it time and again when my focus needs to be corrected. Here is a brief synopsis of that chapter. "Learn to get along and work together. Rejoice in the Lord. Do not worry about anything. Pray about everything. Thank God for what He has done. Let the peace of God keep your hearts and minds. Think on the good things. Learn how to be content wherever you are. Believe you can do all things through Christ. Realize that God will supply everything you need." Hebrews 11 is the Hall of Faith Chapter in the Bible. When your life is over, will something you said or did be worthy of going in the appendix?

Trust Your Heart, Try Your Wings, Be willing To Fail

The fear of failure has kept many a person from becoming all that God intended them to be. Those who are risk takers for God are not in the middle of the pack. They are always out front or off by themselves. If you have prayed earnestly and your heart is leading you in a certain direction, go for it. It is always wise to seek godly counsel, but faith is often described as "a leap in the dark." I would rather call it a "step of faith" or "act of obedience." If you feel led to follow your heart, try your wings. Remember the words of the Apostle Paul, "Faithful is he that called you, who also will do it" (I Thessalonians 5:24). If God is leading, He will give you the ability to do the job. The reason many people never try anything special is that they fear they will embarrass themselves or disappoint others. Trying something and failing is almost an expected fact in the discovery of some new thing. The key is to refuse to stay down. Get up and try again. You now know something that will not work so you can scratch that possibility off of your list.

Walk in the Fullness of the Holy Spirit

The Holy Spirit has been sent by our Lord to help us on our journey. The word "Comforter" in the New Testament means "One called alongside to help." The early Apostles were an amazement to the religious leaders in their day because of the filling of the Holy Spirit and the power He brought to their lives. . ." (Acts 4:8-14, 31). If we quench or grieve the Holy Spirit, His power will not be effective in our lives. We are to walk in the Spirit and seek the filling of the Spirit on a regular basis.

Never Quit Until God Calls You Home

Some of the greatest works done for God have been accomplished by people of faith in their later years. We should never quit until the job is done. If God gives you extra strength and energy in later life, He must have some things left for you to do. We are never too young or too old to do something special for God. Remember the words of the Apostle Paul to the Philippian church, "Being confident of this very thing, that he which hath begun a good work in you will perform it until the day of Jesus Christ" (Philippians 1:6). What God starts, He finishes. You are almost home. Don't quit now!

Being Thankful

Chapter XI
Being Thankful For Who You Are

Early this morning, I was at the hospital to celebrate the arrival of a new baby into a family which has loved him for months and who eagerly welcomed him into their world. As usual, folks crowded close to the window to gain a better look at the newest member of the family. The normal comments were made. "He has his daddy's mouth." "He has long fingers like his mother." "He has a good pair of lungs like the rest of the family." There is nothing to compare to the birth of a new baby and the joy and pride which he brings to the family.

Have you ever considered how God might have felt when we entered this world? Of course He knew all about us long before we were born. However, if God were to say something to His angels when we were born, this is what I would like for Him to have said about me: "He has a heart like mine." Remember we were made in the image and likeness of God. We have the potential to bring pleasure to our God who might say of one of us, "This is my son in whom I am well pleased."

A Realistic Acceptance

The Psalmist said, "I am fearfully and wonderfully made!" Can you say something similar and mean it? In order to be thankful for who you are, you must come to a realistic acceptance of Who made you, and that He had a specific plan in mind when He put you together. Either you believe that this world and everything in it just happened, or that there is a Creator who has a perfect plan. I personally think it takes more faith to believe in the theory of evolution than to believe "In the beginning God created the heaven and the earth." Being yourself as God made you is one way to agree that God knows best. Are you at peace with who you were made to be?

Unwise Comparisons

The Apostle Paul told the Christians at Corinth that it is unwise to compare yourself to anyone else. ". . . that ye might learn in us not to think of men above that which is written, that no one of you be puffed up for one against another. For who maketh thee to differ from another? And what hast thou that thou didst not receive? Now if thou didst receive it, why dost thou glory, as if thou hadst not received it?" (I Corinthians 4:6-7). Being who God made you should never lead you to look down on others or cause you to think you are better than others. We often use the phrase, "That is like comparing apples to oranges." This is even truer when we try to compare one individual to another. The spirit of competition is too strong on this earth. In God's plan, everybody wins when we do things His way.

Guard Against Pride

One of the key evils in this world is pride. Pride originated in the heart of Lucifer which drove him to become the evil one known as the Devil and Satan. One of the deceptions of a sinful human being is to think of himself more highly than he should. This was clearly demonstrated in the parable of the Pharisee and the Publican. "Two men went up to the temple to pray; the one a Pharisee, and the other a publican. The Pharisee stood and prayed thus with himself, God, I thank thee, that I am not as other men are, extortioners, unjust, adulterers, or even as this publican. I fast twice in the week, I give tithes of all that I possess. And the publican, standing afar off, would not lift up so much as his eyes unto heaven, but smote upon his breast, saying, God be merciful to me a sinner. I tell you, this man went down to his house justified rather than the other: for everyone that exalteth himself shall be abased; and he that humbleth himself shall be exalted" (Luke 18:10-14).

Humility and meekness are two virtues which are presented in the Bible as very desirable. Being thankful for who you are should be expressed in the spirit of those two traits. Humility acknowledges a higher authority while meekness speaks of strength under control. The best picture of meekness I have discovered is of a stallion which has been trained to obey its rider. A well-trained horse will move at the slightest touch of the reins on its neck. That horse has lost none of its power but it accepts its rider as its master. Would it not be great if you and I could learn to let God neck-rein us on our journey through this world?

Made To Praise the Lord

The most frequently mentioned command in the Bible is, "Praise ye the Lord!" Everything that has breath is designed to praise the Lord. One true sign of personal development is to lose our focus on ourselves and to become captivated by the wonderful attributes of our God. You are unique and one of a kind. You can bring certain things to the throne room of God that no one else can bring. Think of yourself as a flower in a beautiful bouquet placed in the presence of God to adore His heavenly temple. You should bring beauty, fragrance and praise to the Lord our God.

As you learn the freedom of being yourself, you can begin the exciting journey of developing into the person God so lovingly designed you to be.